Skyscratchers and Cloudcatchers

Chicago to Cologne

I0419272

by

Cheryl Chapman

and

Josef Mahlmeister

Bibliographic information published by the Deutsche Nationalbibliothek

The Deutsche Nationalbibliothek lists this publication
in the Deutsche Nationalbibliografie;
detailed bibliographic data are available on the Internet
at http://dnb.dnb.de .

* * *

For all of the students of Cheryl, Barbara and JoJo:
DREAM BIG AND TRAVEL!

*

1. Edition – Cologne / Chicago | June 2015

The exact printing information you will find at the last page.
CreateSpace, Charleston SC

ISBN-13: 978-1-514-65141-4
ISBN-10: 1-514-65141-6

From Chicago to Cologne and Cologne to Chicago

Dear Frau Schmitz and Pen Pal Friends,

Let us introduce you to our Chicago-style skyline. We all wrote this poem together.

Sincerely,
Mrs. Castle's Class

Skyscrapers and Cloudscratchers

An immensity of stone
These towers wanted to be a mountain range when they grew up,
As if the hands of people could build one.
We play (at their mighty feet) with the clouds:
Peek-a-boo!

Smiling, we get beamed up in elevators,
To the top of our immense city.
Our heads, immensities of dizziness,
As we look down at the human ants
And their little toy cars.

We, too, want to scratch the clouds,
Scrape the skies,
When we grow up.

The skyline view, from Chicago´s Navy Pier and the Windy Waves of Lake Michigan

Dear Mrs. Castle and Pen Partner Friends,
The Dom of Cologne is our most famous site for tourists.
Maybe, the first time you see it, it will remind you of a big, stone, dragon.
Our class put our Josef's story into a poem!

Yours,
Frau Schmitz's Class

The Dom of Cologne

When I was little
What I saw first from the tour boat
Was a giant dragon with a long tail,
Dangerous, rising, with his two ears scratching at the clouds.

My class walked to the front of him.
We could see his hungry eyes staring down
Ready to eat all the tourists who walked into his mouth.
The teacher said, "The Three Kings are buried inside!"
Oh, how sad, I thought, *he ate them all up*.
"And now we, too, may go inside," the teacher said.
To be eaten? I thought, *not me!*
But, our teacher went in, and so did we, and...

There I was in the belly of that dragon.
I wandered about the insides of that humongous cathedral.
Gothic, they called it and I looked up to see ribs.
Its windows were walls made of light, shining through dragon skin.

A very old lady knelt, and lit a candle,
A light in the dragon's belly. She pointed to a door.
We tiptoed over to it and climbed and climbed and climbed up
533 spiral staircase steps, past the bell called Thick Peter,
All the way to the top of the world of Cologne
Where we could see trains and boats and ant people.
And I whispered into the wind,
Into my wonderful dragon's ear,
"I'll never be afraid of you again!"

Dragon tail and ears…oops, actually the Rhine bridge from the trains, and the back of the Dom.

Street view from the front of the Dom.
Notice the scaffold on the left steeple.
They are always restoring it.
The steeple on the right holds the viewing area.

Dear Frau Schmitz and Pen Pal Friends,
  Chicago sits at the shores of beautiful Lake Michigan.
We play with the waves and with the words, and yes,
another name for our lake is "The Sweetwater Sea."
We tell our friends, Terrence and Brian, that the diamonds aren't real,
and that it isn't the ocean, really, but they still doesn't believe us!
                                    Best wishes,
                                    Mrs. Castle's Class

Lake Michigan

lake forever
ripples rippling
white caps rapping
slapping sloshing
timeless blue lake music gnoshing
moving carpet of silk and diamonds
softly rising falling rising falling
covering the shivers deep below

i bet i could walk on that carpet
yes walk
breathing in the fresh wet wind
i bet i could collect all those diamonds
yes, i bet my friends and i could start here
on the sands, skyline to our backs
and walk and walk and walk
upon these silky ripples
all the way to that ocean out there.

Our view of Lake Michigan from a skyscraper

Dear Mrs. Castle and Pen Partners,
our river, the Rhine, leads to the ocean. But the water that smells like flowers is named after our town, Cologne. The boys in our class do not like this smelly water, and sometimes they joke about it, as you will see in this poem.

-By the Boys ☺

P.S. But we really do like chocolate!

A Perfume Factory Called 4711

Forty-seven and eleven
Not forty-six, not number 10.
Girls like this smelly water of Cologne.
Why? We don't know the answer,
So please, don't ask us boys!
Find a girl instead!

She will tell you that the water called "Cologne" is fine,
To wear, but not to drink.
We boys will take you to any Rhine River bridge and say,
Look, do you see that river? It is not water!
It is cologne! Our beautiful, sparkling, Rhine!
It's fine! For girls! Don't drink it though!

We are tricksters,
But do not trick us; we will not fall for it!
If you come to us boys and say,
Here, have some Rhine, it's fine?
We will not drink it.

We will certainly not wear it.
And now? You know why!

Children looking at the Rhine River, Hohenzollern Bridge, and boats.

Stollwerck Chocolate Museum

A museum of chocolate! Live! In Cologne!
Trees! Beans! Machines! Schokolade!

But the sweets will not live to be very old... - No!

All the visitors will try to stake a claim on the newborn nuggets,
tastier than gold, isn't it true? - Yes!

We will eat up all the samples! But guess what we take home for souvenirs?
Cavities! - Oww!

Dear Frau Schmitz's Class,

    We are learning about haiku poems now so we are now sending you some of our autumn in two poems!

Smiles from your friends in Frau Schmitz's Class!

The leaves leave the trees
And the windy winds wind through
Falls-Farmers' markets.

And then we made another one :

Leaves

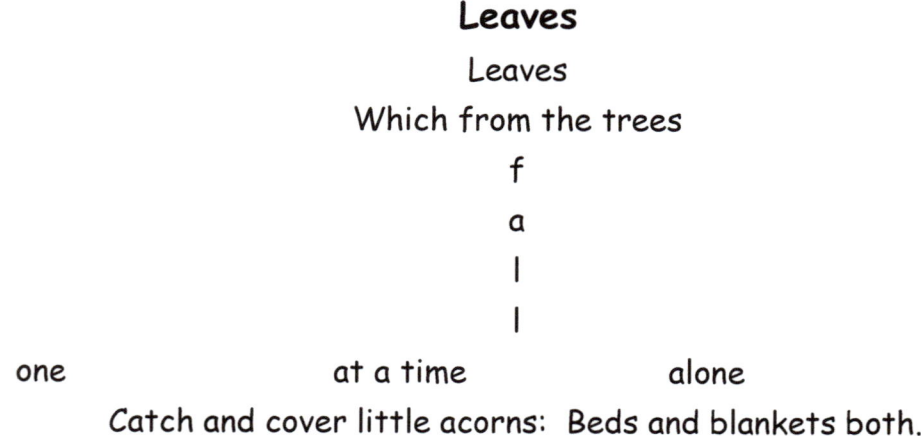

Leaves
Which from the trees
f
a
l
l
one   at a time   alone
Catch and cover little acorns: Beds and blankets both.

Dear Mrs. Castle's Class,
one Saturday, we all got together and took a ride on the bike path to the
"Stadtwald," or city forest. It´s amazing!

Smiles back,
Frau Schmitz's Class

*A Poem Built for Two Riders**

Cool, cool, cool breeze   **Smooth Riding**

Pedal now, pedal and zoom

Pedal through the October noon

Happy biking, wheel hiking **Windy swept places, windy swept faces**

Pedal left, pedal right

All day long and into night

Past buildings of glass   **Past meadow grasses**

Powerful   **Flowerful**

Pedal fast, pedal slow

Pedal, pedal, pedal so…

Quick! Dodge that duck!   **Hey! Lose that goose!**

Don't smush the seagull!   **Our chain is loose!**

Finally! Let's stop this poem and go fishing.

Bait the line and start the wishing.

*Voice one

Voice two

Together

And this is a path that runs through Cologne!

P.S.

We got hungry after the bike rides. We are learning about dinosaurs and carnivores. And how to say potato in lots of different languages. Have you ever cooked potato pancakes in science class? We have! Here in Cologne, we call them Reibekuchen or Rievkooche. You just grate the potatoes, add eggs, quark, salt and pepper and fry them up! And this is our story about it. In a poem, of course!

Cologne's famous potato pancakes - Reibekuchen!

Dinovores

In anybody's language "Pterodactyl" is the same.
Wouldn't it be better though If each country gave Pterry her very own name?

In English, Potatodactyl sounds just delicious.
A German Kartoffelpuffer-Raptor? Ach, so nutritious!
In Italy or Portugal a Patatadactyle could really fly,
And in France, Pomme-de-terre-dactyls would finally rule the sky.

But let's not complain about the name, Dinosaur pancakes? Let's gobble more!
If we eat them all up we are not to blame
It's the right thing to do if you are a dinovore!

Dear Frau Schmitz and Class,
Here in Chicago we are preparing for the holidays. So, we send best wishes inside of this poem!

Cheers! Mrs. Castle's Class

Deep Bright Winter: Celebrate!

Here in Chicago
When the weather turns cold
The days grow shorter
And our streets bright as gold!

Chicagolanders celebrate in oodles of ways
With surprises and food and music and plays.
Wintertime is family time,
With a holiday from school,
With ice skates and hot chocolate.

Winter is cool, not cruel!
We celebrate in oodles of ways,
And we send you best wishes
For the New Year and for fun and snowy days!

At the ice rink – Chicago in wintertime

Dear Mrs. Castle's Class,
now that the holidays are over we must celebrate Karneval!
Our whole school will march in a parade! In America, kids dress up
for Halloween. Here? It's Karneval!

Kölle Alaaf / Long Live Karneval!
Frau Schmitz's Class

Decisions, Decisions...

Let's go to the Karneval parade together
We'll enjoy Cologne's famous rainy weather.
If we watch the parade we'll catch enough candy to last for years.
If we march in the parade we'll get lots of cheers.
Did we tell you that Karneval lasts all night?
Shout "Kölle Alaaf" and you'll be all right!

Each child wonders what to wear
From funny feet to multi-colored hair:
Clown? Tiger? Wizard? Witch?
Shall I make a personality switch?
Superhero? Cat? Troll? Elf?
Or just go to Karneval as myself?

Feathers, sequins, sparkles, glue
I'll make a mask and tell everyone I'm you!
I look in the mirror – imagine a vision
I'm a Karneval star - that's my decision!

Each year we dance and march – we do this 'til we're old
Please share your candy and your prizes
But not your Karneval cold!...
Ka-choo!

The famous Cologne Karneval

Dear Mrs. Castle's Class,
And now that Karneval is over, may we present: Springtime!!! We love how Americans call our "Frühling" "Spring!" "Frühling" means early, a beginning, and yes, the sun does come up earlier…and the green begins, but really? Let's go with English on this one!

Springing-Jumping-Cartwheeling!
Frau Schmitz's Class

Boing! - Boing! - Ouch!

Ah…the first day of Spring!
Spring? A fine English word!
Spring means jumping:
We *spring* from a bungee bridge
We *spring* from a diving board
Showers *spring* from the clouds
It feels so good to survive when we *spring*!

For springtime in Germany we say the word "Early."
Too early in life for anything
As dangerous and fun as springing
Like a wild little kid or elf…
Doing cartwheels in the sky
So happy that the icy cold winter blanket
Is finally melting away.

Yes, we will be so happy, springing in springtime
Boing! - Boing! - Boing!
"Ouch!" we cry, "this ground's as hard as ice!"
When we land on our bottoms,

So in English, perhaps, it would be more honest and true
To change the word from "Spring" to "Boing! - Boing! - Crash!"
Then we little wild children and elves
Might be more careful of our little wild selves!

The magical springtime flowers at Flora, the best gardens in Cologne

Dear Frau Schmitz's Class,

In our horrible rainy cold spring weather, our teachers like to take us on field trips – indoors! So, we went to the Art Institute, and there, we saw some stained glass windows that **Marc Chagall** gave to Chicago! Our art teacher let us try to capture the artwork in a poem. In English, you must spell the color blue as **B-L-U-E**, but the **blues** in these windows are so much more than just blue – so, we call this poem **Bloo**!

Creatively yours,
Mrs. Castle's Class

BLOO

When the world is bloo
Sky bloo, crystal bloo
Candle bloo, morning glory bloo

And bloo zooms everywhere ...
Into the sounds and noises and music
And dances and literature
And plays and pictures
And the softness of stones
And the echoes of stories
And the air is bloo blown kisses
Or wet bloo splashes
And everything glows like
Mysterious bloo ghosty ghosts.

Only then does the bloo truth turn real:
Sand is jewels
The world is a poem.

Dear Mrs. Castle's Class,
do you have recycling machines in Chicago? We have them, and they eat a *lot*!

Guten Appetit!
Frau Schmitz's Class

Earth Day Cake!

In Cologne Breakfast is a most important meal.
First, you should eat
A hot water heater
So that you will not be cold all day.

Then you should eat a refrigerator
So that you will not be hot all day.
Also, you should eat the motor of a car
So that you can be on the go all day.

You may have this with coffee cups,
Soda pop cans, or teacups.
Breakfast should never be light,
But heavy – if you are a trash compactor,

This kind of meal will be just right.
Of course, if you are a kid
And that's what you plan to stay,
Just stick with eggs and little rolls 'cause
Breakfast won't be so disgusting that way!

Dear Frau Schmitz's Class,
Spring is coming. This means testing season. Some kids like tests, but this poem does not!

High Fives!
Mrs. Castle's Class

The Poem versus The Test

Every spring in Chicago
Teachers try hard
To teach their students to take tests.
Special tests that all the kids in Chicago,
No, in Illinois, no, in America,
No, the tests that all kids in the whole wide universe,
must take.

Now, I am a good writer.
I am a good thinker.
And I want to write, right now, this:
That I am a good little poem
And I am here to say that
I would rather plant a vegetable garden
Or draw a bird with detailed feathers
Or design a mall out of blocks
Or play Rapunzel at recess
Or write a million more poems
Than have to learn how to take the springtime test.

Kids working and learning in the prairie garden they planted after school…

Dear Frau Schmitz's Class,

We are learning some words in German. Yes, the names of your bugs. But they are tongue twisters for us! So, can you say our poem fast without breaking *your* tongues?

Good luck,
Mrs. Castle's Class

German Lesson

There is something bugging us.
From English to German
The names of the bugs twist and turn and break our tongues.
Why can't bugs have simple names like Hermione or Herman?

Schmetterling is butterfly: Letterschming flutterby!
Marienkäfer is ladybug: Karienmaefer badylug!
(And anyway, where is the gentleman bug?)
Libelle is dragonfly, so bilelle fly-on-by,

Fliege is fly, so Fliege Schmliege fliegst weg, shoo, fly, go away!
Stechmueche (ouch!) is mosquito, so,
Stechmueche Mechstuecke, (ouch!), mosquito bandito (ouch!).
What? You bit me on the leg? Bam-pow! Go!

My tongue is now broken, twisted and kaputt
My leg is all itchy right down to the foot
Hey, Mr. Hummer, you bumblebee, you, stay away from these toes.
Bzzzzzzzzzzzzzzzzzt!   Ow! You stung my nose?

At last! "Ow" is easy to say in German and English,
Always remember to scream "Ow" if you get a sting-lish!

Dear Mrs. Castle's Class,

now we will teach you some more German! "Der" rhymes with "there," "Die" rhymes with "see," and "Dass" rhymes with "boss." And der, die, and das all mean "the." In Germany, ever since you are born, you learn the proper form of "the" to put in front of all your nouns! And "sagt" sounds like "zockt" and of course it means "says."

Tschüss! "Bye!"
Frau Schmitz's Klasse

Learning German for Kids and Pets!

In Chicago a child says "Hello."
In Cologne, the child is "das Kind" and says "Guten Tag."
The dog says "Bow-Wow," Der Hund sagt wau-wau.
The cat says "Meow," die Katze sagt "Miau."
The cow says "Moo," die Kuh sagt "Muh."

The chicken says "Cluck-cluck-cluck," das Huhn sagt "Gack-gack-gack."
And the rooster says "Cock-a-doodle-do," und der Hahn sagt "Kikeriki!"
In any language animals can yack-yack-yack,
But Teddy bears are silent
And we kids just love them back!

Dear Frau Schmitz's Class,
Do you have an end-of-the-year picnic? We did! And we invite you for next year!

Your Chicago Friends,

Mrs. Castle's Class

Class Picnic

Our bugs and butterflies
Today – they are dancing
Flying buzzing dashing around our noses.

Today – we are lying
Dreaming, cloud-watching, letting ourselves go
In the green grass, prairie and fountains at Millennium Park!
Today, they are congratulating us –
Dragonflies, ladybugs, butterflies
Up in the blue skies.

Today – they are the invited guests
Of our school's party
Which once a year happens to happen right here!

Today – we celebrate and are happy all together
And the long, long, day lasts forever.

Today – we laugh, eat and
Drink until it's very late.
And the lightning bugs blink: Go home!

Today – we close our eyes
And dream of what a great picnic that was!
We wish you were here. Maybe next year?

Happy "Kids" at Navy Pier

And fun under the "Bean" at Millennium Park

Dear Mrs. Castle's Class,
we had a great picnic, and the journey was as much fun as the park!

☺ Summertime smiles,
Frau Schmitz's Class

Directions

To have a great class picnic in Cologne you must:
Pack a lunch, go to school, buddy up!
Take a walk, find a train - all aboard!
Ride, ride, ride
All the way to the River Rhine.

Off the train and all aboard the ferry!
Cross the Rhine, Bye-bye ferry,
Time to dine! Munch your lunch! Playtime!

Soccer, swings, climbing ropes
Scavenger hunts, hiking, singing, sliding,
More songs, more hikes, more hunts, more soccer
Even the teachers must play all day!

And then? Backwards!
All aboard the ferry,
Cross the Rhine, Bye-bye ferry,
All off the ferry and all aboard the train.
Ride ride ride and everybody out!
Walk back to school, go inside,
And wish we could do this again tomorrow…

Cologne kids picnic on the Rhine River

Our Multi-Culti Happily Ever Afterly Poem

Sky scratchers	Cloud catchers
Museums and malls	Chocolate waterfalls
Magnificent Miles	Glockenspiel smiles
Skyscraper mountains	Splashing wet fountains
Views from up high	Shopping in the sky
Fields for sports	Roman towers and forts
Supermarkets	Farmers' Markets
Hot dogs and fries are good eats	Like Wurst & Pommes Frites
Have some rootbeer	Apfelschorle over here
Coffee shops treats	Konditorei sweets
Navy Pier to explore	Rhein Park's lovely shore
El-Trains galore	U-Bahn's really roar
Show us some more!	Yes, more, more, more!

Museums full of science, history, art, all the stories of people
Bridges, city halls, waterfronts, fireworks, many a tall steeple
Sculptures of horses and heroes abound
Festivals and celebrations happen all the year 'round.

How can we be homesick for a place we've never been before?
Let's be like our poems and cross over the ocean
Exchange "Hello´s!" and "Guten Tag´s!" in "Happy greeting!"
Let's look forward to a day when poetry pals will be meeting.

And… this is:

THE END

or: A Start of a very long and World-Wide Friendship?! :-)

www.ingramcontent.com/pod-product-compliance
Lightning Source LLC
Chambersburg PA
CBHW060808290526
45792CB00005BA/1561